TANZANIA IN AFRICA

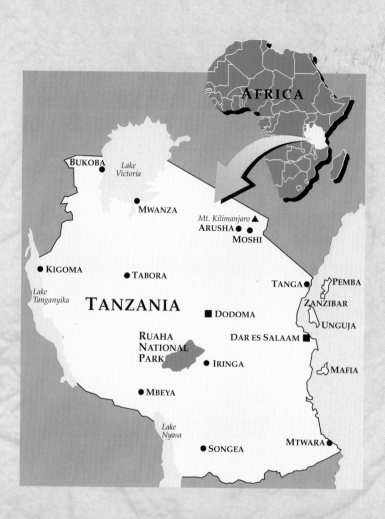

Published for:

TANZANIA NATIONAL PARKS (TANAPA)
PO Box 3134, Arusha
Tanzania

by:

AFRICAN PUBLISHING GROUP (INTERNATIONAL)
PO Box BW 350, Harare
Zimbabwe

First published 2000

ISBN: 1-77916-008-9
© APG. Pictures as credited. Maps and published edition APG
Photographic credits: All David Martin except pages 18, 25, (Paul Hicks);
19, 22, 41, 43, 44 (bottom), 47 (bottom), 47 (top), 51 (right), 52, 53, 54 (top)
and 55 (Neil Baker); 33 (Charmer, Paris) 42 and cover (Nick Greaves);
backcover (TANAPA/Christopher Ratier).
Edited by: Phyllis Johnson
Readers: Lota Melamari, Mtango Mtahiko, Peter Fox, Christopher Fox,
Robert Glen, Neil Baker and Mike Patterson
Design: Joe Byrne, Harare
Origination and Printing: Creda Communications, Johannesburg

TANZANIA IN AFRICA

INTRODUCTION

Ruaha National Park is located in Tanzania west of the Iringa highlands. The ecosystem makes it one of the country's most outstanding wilderness areas containing an excellent park with an expanding all-weather road network, good accommodation, very different faces in the wet and dry seasons and abundant wildlife.

Ruaha National Park

The park takes its name from the Great Ruaha River. The word "ruaha" is a linguistic corruption of the word "luvaha" which means a river, brook or stream in the language of the Wahehe people who live in the vicinity.

The Wahehe name for the river is "Lyambangari" which is still used by some of the older people living in and around Iringa town.

The Great Ruaha River begins in the high catchment mountains which feed it through the Usangu wetlands 50 km southwest of the park.

Much of Ruaha National Park was once the home of the Wahehe people who numerically still dominate Iringa town and the surrounding area. Long before their arrival, scattered groups of hunter-gatherers temporarily resided in the area. In the Mwagusi Sand River area, anthropologists call them Kosi Samba.

Twenty km south of Iringa town on the Mbeya road an important stone age site was discovered in 1957 at Isimila. Stone Age tools and weapons found at the site have been dated as being 60,000 years old. Dramatic sandstone columns stand nearby as mute sentinels marking the course of a bygone river.

One of many Stone Age tools found at Isimila

The Wahehe people, armed only with spears and other early weapons and led by the formidable Chief Mkwawa, spearheaded Tanzanian resistance to German colonialism after 1885.

Opposite page: The stark sandstone columns at Isimila

RUAHA NATIONAL PARK
GAME VIEWING ROADS

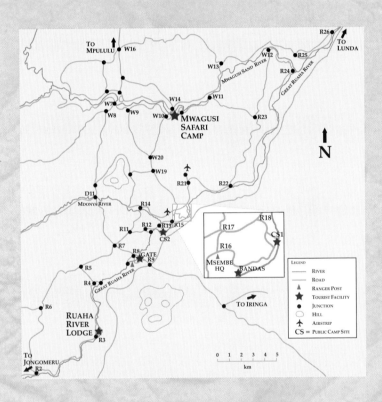

Map courtesy of Friends of Ruaha Society
P.O.Box 7589 Dar es Salaam, Tanzania.

German monument to their patrol

The Wahehe's chilling war-cry "hee-hee" reverberated through the region's granite hills and they routed and killed a ten-man German patrol near Iringa.

A price was placed on Chief Mkwawa's head but, after almost four more years of guerrilla war, he committed suicide in June 1898 rather than be captured.

His head was taken to Germany and displayed at the Bremen Anthropological Museum until 1964 when it was returned to his grandson, the late Chief Adam Sapi, the speaker of independent Tanganyika's first parliament. The skull is now buried in the Sapi family cemetery near Iringa.

Sign in Swahili points to the monument commemorating the 100th anniversary of Chief Mkwawa's death

In 1910, the German colonial administration, before that country's defeat in the First World War, created the Saba River Game Reserve. This was re-gazetted as the Rungwa Game Reserve in 1946 by the British who had been given a mandate to run Tanganyika by the League of Nations (forerunner of the United Nations).

Ruaha National Park was formally gazetted as a protected area in 1964, three years after Tanganyika became independent from Britain. The park encompassed the southeastern portion of the Rungwa Game Reserve.

The park lies in central Tanzania and is 130 km (81 miles) from Iringa town. It is 625 km (391 miles) from the commercial capital, Dar es Salaam, 430 km (269 miles) from Morogoro and 621 km (388 miles) from the Zambian border.

The number of visitors to the park is increasing. Twice a week (Tuesday and Thursday) Air Malawi flies to the southwestern Tanzanian town of Mbeya where passengers can connect to the Tanzanian carrier, Precision Air, who have a thrice weekly service (Tuesday, Thursday and Sunday) from Dar es Salaam to Iringa and Mbeya returning the same day.

From Dar es Salaam there are charter services to the dirt airstrip near the park headquarters at Msembe. Enquires for these can be made through Coastal Travel.

At present Ruaha National Park has two main types of tourist accommodation. Both belong to the innovative Fox family (Foxtreks) who come from nearby Mufindi. One, which is divided into three camps, is Ruaha River Lodge run by Peter and Sarah Fox. This is located on the banks of the Great Ruaha River ten km upstream from the park entrance.

Twelve km to the north of the park entrance is Mwagusi Safari Camp located on the bank of the Mwagusi Sand River which is a ribbon of sand in the dry season and a flowing torrent during the rains.

The camp has eight well located en-suite tents, accommodates only 16 people and is an authentic and mildly rustic safari experience run by Christopher Fox who, in the positive sense of the word, is very much a bushman.

Christopher Fox and his friend, Constantine, a mature bull whose tusks weigh around 45 kg each. Visitors should not do the same thing to this or any other animal

Sites for two other tented camps have been awarded to the Selous Safari Company at Jongomero and to Coastal Travel at Upper Mdonya.

No amount of words can prepare the visitor for the magnificence of Ruaha. Its very remoteness is perhaps its greatest charm. It exists untouched and apart; Tanzania's second largest park (after Serengeti) covering an area of 10,300 sq km. Ruaha remains Africa of the imagination: very few tourists and even fewer cars.

Nor, despite well-intentioned advice to the contrary, should the visitor be lured into regarding Ruaha as a dry season park to be visited only during May to October when most of the trees are leafless, the countryside a rich golden-yellow and tourism is at its peak.

Egyptian geese hurry past sunburned hippopotamus in the Great Ruaha River

It is true that there are greater numbers of more conspicuous animals during these months slaking their thirst on the Great Ruaha River. But even in the wetter months (which are nothing like those in Europe and North America) the quality and quantity of game is abundant as the park takes on an emerald green hue. And certainly there are fewer visitors.

I arrived at night and was shown to my accommodation in the dark. During the night I heard hippopotamus snorting outside and at dawn I found my chalet was on the banks of the Great Ruaha River.

I would gladly have foregone game viewing that day just to sit on the balcony staring at the river, the pools of water that remained in the dry season, granite rocks, hippopotamus a few metres away and birdlife. The solitude and sheer beauty of Ruaha is simply breathtaking.

The countryside is dramatic. Blue, rolling hills interspersed by flat, open areas of grassland. The Great Ruaha River, which winds for 160 km (100 miles) along the park's southeastern boundary, is fringed by tall acacia, tamarind and wild fig trees. Grotesque, yet simultaneously magnificent, baobab trees are common in the north of the park.

What to take

The short answer is a minimum. Most safari camps have same-day laundry service and three sets of clothes rotated should be more than enough. The clothes should be neutral coloured so you blend in with your surroundings.

It can be cold, particularly at nights and on the dawn drive (not highly recommended by Ruaha operators because of the scarcity of wildlife). So a lightweight sweater or wind-breaker is advised. Long trousers and shirts minimise mosquito and tsetse fly bites. Strong walking shoes or boots, a torch, hat, sun glasses and sun lotions should also be packed.

Binoculars, which many people forget, are essential, particularly for scanning the bush. Reversed they become a microscope. Cameras are optional, some people preferring to simply view. But if you want to take a camera then a sturdy one is recommended with a zoom lens up to 300 mm and slow (100 ASA) film. Do not forget your camera cleaning kit.

Water is generally treated and vegetables are washed so they should be safe. But mosquitoes are a nuisance and you should take repellent and prophylactics. Check what you should use and the frequency with your local doctor. Tsetse fly is another nuisance. But they cause little more than an irritating lump.

Do not be afraid to ask questions. There is no such thing as a silly question; only a silly answer.

Ruaha National Park is the transition zone or meeting point where much of the flora and fauna which distinguishes eastern and southern Africa meets and overlaps. Being able to see greater and lesser kudu, roan and sable antelope in one park is part of Ruaha's special attraction. This is also the southern limit of Grant's gazelle.

Beyond this there are also lion, leopard, cheetah, hunting dog and other predators, large herds of elephant (some tuskless) and some 8,000 giraffe (a local joke holds that Ruaha should be renamed Giraffic Park).

In addition there are abundant plains game such as zebra and impala while hippopotamus and crocodile are numerous along the Great Ruaha River.

Ruaha is part of an ecosystem covering at least 40,000 sq km. The ecosystem encompasses the Rungwa, Kizogo and Muhesi game reserves to the north, Usangu Game Reserve to the immediate south and Lumba Mkwambi (north and south) areas to the east and southeast which have been set aside for hunting and wildlife management.

Maasai giraffe

RUAHA ECOSYSTEM

Ruaha National Park is part of a much larger ecosystem which includes other protected areas. As in most national parks, much of the wildlife which inhabits the area moves across the boundaries at certain seasons of the year in search of food and water

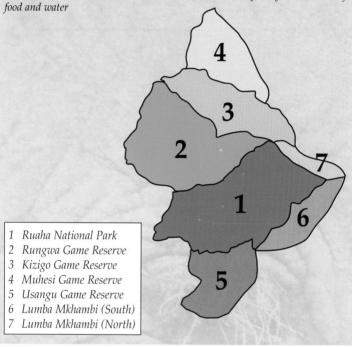

1   Ruaha National Park
2   Rungwa Game Reserve
3   Kizigo Game Reserve
4   Muhesi Game Reserve
5   Usangu Game Reserve
6   Lumba Mkhambi (South)
7   Lumba Mkhambi (North)

Ruaha National Park has four main vegetation zones. Acacia is to be found in the extreme east. Moving southwest, bracystegia woodland and then commiphora come next and there is a small pocket of drypetes in the southwest.

The birdlife is spectacular. Over 440 species have been recorded which is two-thirds the number found in most southern African countries. The park is noted for its significant number of rare migrant Eleanora's falcons which may be seen in December/January.

Despite Ruaha's abundance of different species, a warning is necessary about this particular park – and all parks in Africa. Game viewing in the wild has a lot to do with luck. Nevertheless, and certainly in either the dry or wet seasons, you are assured of seeing game at Ruaha.

But you should always remember that you are not sitting at home in your favourite armchair watching a wildlife film on television that took experts years to make. What you are hearing, seeing, smelling and feeling is Africa with its own special moods and times of the day.

David Martin
Ruaha, January 2000

Lioness

GEOLOGY & CLIMATE

Ruaha National Park is bisected by the Great Ruaha River and lies in the rain shadow of Udzungwa Mountains in the southeast. The park is the southern extension of the Maasai steppes to the north. It is among the most arid of Tanzania's 12 national parks.

Eastern Arc Mountains

The proximity of the 10,000 sq km (6,250 sq miles) Udzungwa Mountains is important for these mountains act as a formidable obstacle to the inland movement of rain clouds from the Indian Ocean.

The Udzungwas are the largest block in the arc which has been described as the "Galapagos Islands of Africa". The Udzungwas and other sections of the eastern arc were formed where the continental shelf was pushed upward by the oceanic shelf.

The eastern arcs 11 geologically separated mountain ranges begin with the Taita Hills in Kenya. Then, in an crescent-shaped broken chain, the arc stretches north to south across Tanzania ending in the Mahenge Hills near the sugar producing Kilombero valley.

Each of the fragmented mountains of the arc encompasses a patchwork of dense tropical forest which attracts the clouds and resulting rain. They also provide the habitat for many unique plant, animal, bird, amphibian, reptile and insect (including butterfly) communities.

Clouds break up on the Udzungwa Mountains and Ruaha gets the overspill with its annual rainfall being somewhat less than the amount deposited by the clouds on the western side of Udzungwa Mountains National Park (UMNP).

Opposite page: The Great Ruaha River provides the park's lifeblood

Rainfall

Ruaha, in common with most of Tanzania, receives its most intensive rains from January to May with a short gap in February and light "cleaning up" showers after the rains. Once it was customary to talk of two rainy seasons in Tanzania.

These were the short rain (vuli in Swahili) between October and November and the long and more intensive rains (masika) from March to May. The short rains often fail while the intensity of the long rains varies enormously. Today some meteorologists refer to the Tanzanian cycle as "single season rains".

The total rainfall at Ruaha is less disparate than in the neighbouring Udzungwa Mountains where the amount can vary from 2,000 mm (80 inches) in the east of the park on the Indian Ocean side to 600 mm (24 inches) in the western rain shadow closer to Ruaha and Iringa.

Rainfall in Ruaha National Park averages around 500 mm (20 inches) at Msembe in the valley to 800 mm (32 inches) above the escarpment in the miombo wooded area.

Maximum average temperatures just before the rains can rise to 40 degrees centigrade by day and drop to 25 degrees centigrade at night. In the cooler month of July the temperature drops from 30 degrees centigrade in the day to 15 degrees centigrade at night. Six degrees centigrade has been recorded at Mwagusi at 0500 hours in June.

The best months to visit Ruaha (unless you are an avid bird watcher or butterfly collector when January to May is preferred) is in the dry season from May to November. Some of the 1,200 km (750 miles) of tracks may be closed during the rains although common game is still abundant.

In October and November it is beginning to get hotter. But these two months have the merit of spectacular lightning and thunder storms which overshadow the babbling of the rivers.

The base of Ruaha is probably 450 to 650 million years old. Upward faulting of the earth's crust resulting in buckling which created the mountains. Downward faulting created the Great Rift Valley which runs through the African continent for 4,800 km (3,000 miles) from Ethiopia to the Zambezi River.

The Great Ruaha River, the valley of which is an extension of the Great Rift Valley, eventually joins the Rufiji River before emptying into the Indian Ocean opposite Mafia Island, a fishing and diving haven, which is a Tanzanian offshore island.

The area is a fusion of the ancient Mozambique shield of Usagaran biotite gneiss (a common rock-forming mineral of the mica group) combined with coarse grained, banded, crystalline rock and Archaean granites (a geological period over 2,000 million years ago referring to ancient basement rocks). Weathering and erosion thereafter sculpted today's landscape.

The majority of the Ruaha National Park is dominated by a plateau which is roughly 100 m higher in the northeastern parts, rising slightly further in the southwest.

A heron flies over the bare rocks and few pools left in the river

Only 20 percent of the park is along Great Ruaha River although this is the part of Ruaha most people visit because of its better developed road network, accommodation and good game viewing. Further attractions in this area are the granite *kopjes* and balancing rocks.

The central spine or roof of Ruaha runs south-north across the length of the park with rivers beginning just above the escarpment. These flow into the Great Ruaha River which marks the eastern boundary of the park, or into the Mzombe River which forms the western boundary.

These two rivers contained the only perennial water once found in the park. However, in recent years towards the end of the dry season, the Great Ruaha River has been reduced to a series of pools abounding with fish, hippopotamus and crocodile.

Chiriwindi Hill across the grass plains

The reduced flow of the river is of concern to consumers of Tanzanian-generated electricity as well as conservationists. The Mtera dam, into which the Great Ruaha River flows, and the Kidatu dam further downstream, were constructed in the late 1970s and early 1980s to generate electricity for 75 percent of the country including Dar es Salaam.

Beyond Ruaha's rivers and swamps lies a well-wooded and undulating plain which rises to the high points of Ndatambulwa 1,630 m (5,379 feet) in the south and Igawira 1,100 m (3,630 feet) in the west. In the west of Ruaha accessed via Makinde or Jongomeru, the hills rise to around 1,800 m (5,940 feet) and form part of the Isunkavyola plateau.

Into these highland and riverine environments sculpted over millions of years, fit the diverse habitats that provide the homes to species of mammals, birds, butterflies and other insects, fish, amphibians and reptiles which draw people to the park.

Like humans, all wild species have their favourite places or delicacies when they eat out. Elephants, who can dramatically change their environment, are catholic in their habitat requirements and are found throughout the park. But they do require water daily, preferably fresh, shade from the heat of the day, and a wide variety of graze and browse species.

Giraffe, who are predominantly browsers, prefer acacia. It is the absence of preferred acacia species in some parts of northern Tanzania such as Ngorongoro crater that in turn leads to the absence of giraffe which are common elsewhere. Buffalo, which are grazers like domestic cows, readily eat mature grass usually avoiding areas where the grass has been trampled or overgrazed. They tend to be more selective in the rainy rather than dry season.

Predators, for obvious reasons, are to be found where their prey species feed and, given the choice, impala and zebra prefer new grass in open country not far from water. Klipspringer and rock hyrax will be seen on the *kopjes* and rocks and not the plains.

If you pause and think logically about where you are most likely to find a given species all you have to do is know the frequency with which they drink, whether they prefer open, dry, riverine or rocky country, which food they prefer, their need for shade and other habits. The study of animal behaviour provides the answer to many of these questions.

In the same way you would not first look for an addict of Indian food in a French restaurant, you would not look for a zebra in thick forest far from water.

Into all the niches created by geology and the environment various species fit. Water and soil determine the type of vegetation which grows in an area and this in turn determines the species which exist there.

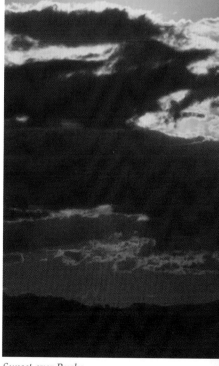

Sunset over Ruaha

INTERACTION OF THE SPECIES

The underlying rock formation, soil, rain, sun, wind and shade all conspire to determine where given plant species grow. This in turn generally predicates where mammals and other species feed, drink and rest in their ecological niches – and therefore where you are most likely to see them.

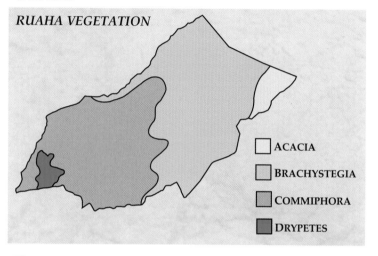

RUAHA VEGETATION

- ACACIA
- BRACHYSTEGIA
- COMMIPHORA
- DRYPETES

The vegetation of the area is particularly interesting as it is the southernmost point for plants such as evergreens, thorny shrubs and annual grasses.

The *Brachystegia* zone of Ruaha also includes the most northerly distribution of examples of *miombo* (the Swahili word for *Brachystegia*) species normally found further south, these are mostly legumes and associated perennial grasses.

As such, Ruaha is a halfway house or meeting point of plant and other species from the north and south of the sub-continent.

A total of over 1,650 plant species have been recorded in the park, the majority of them flowering.

Opposite page: A giraffe framed by hole in a baobab tree

Eulophica zeyheri

The drive to Ruaha National Park over a good all-weather road leads through villages from Iringa and you are in the park for eight km before you come to the entrance gate at Ibuguziwa where the entry fee is paid.

Just after the entry gate a concrete and metal bridge spans the Great Ruaha River. After crossing the bridge you can turn left at the first junction (R8) and head back to the river down a small track to the hippopotamus pool through typical riverine woodland.

The hippopotamus population of Ruaha is impressive. So are the number of other mammals. During five days in February in Ruaha

Ruaha entry sign

I encountered a herd of at least 300 elephant, hundreds of giraffe, scores of greater kudu (all but four female, the males having headed for the hills), and innumerable zebra, waterbuck, impala and dikdik.

In one 24-hour period I saw two packs of hunting dogs numbering fifteen and eight near Mwagusi

Safari Camp and at Jongomeru, three groups of lion and, fleetingly, leopard who have a predilection in Ruaha for the Herculean task of hauling their kills up massive baobabs.

Baobabs

The majestic and impressive baobabs are the most easily recognised and photographed of the trees. They have massive silvery trunks and gourd-like fruit (April to May) covered in greyish-velvety hairs. The large hard-shelled fruit is often sold on the roadside by children. The fruit is edible and contains "cream of tartar" used in cooking.

Baobab have waxy white, short-lived and somewhat pungent flowers (November to January) which are pollinated by fruitbats bats and flies while bushbabies like the sweet nectar. The moisture-filled trunks are frequently the site of wild beehives and the holes a nesting place for hornbills.

The leaves are edible and the long fibre strips from the trunks are used for weaving and rope-making. Baobabs are known in Swahili as "mbuyu" meaning "of" or "at" and many villages are called Mbuyuni.

Baobab trees can live for thousands of years and they are associated with legend. They are said to hold up the sky having been planted upside down and the few spindly branches you see

The baobab (Adansonia digitata) tree is almost Ruaha's signature

should be roots. A potion from the bark makes a person strong; a drink from soaked baobab seed, it is said, protects you from crocodiles.

You will notice that many of Ruaha's baobab trees are bark-less for about five metres up their trunks. That is giraffe height and they, as well as elephant and zebra, chew the bark.

Open grasslands and the inevitable cavernous baobabs, some with huge holes sculpted in the middle and a giraffe or some other animal conveniently framed behind in the open space, are commonplace on the eastern side of the park which is also interspersed with riverine vegetation.

The sausage tree, which grows to 18 m, has a rounded crown and is found along water courses. Its greyish-brown, sausage-shaped seed pods are up to a metre in length and baked slices of these are used to ferment beer. The flowers (December to June) are large, unpleasant smelling and dark red. In the tree the flowers are fed on by bats; on the ground they are eaten by both wildlife and domestic stock.

An eagle flies away from a sausage tree (Kigelia africana)

The centre of Ruaha, including the area around the park headquarters at Msembe and the road to Jongomeru, is dominated by *Combretum* and here you may see kudu. The highlands, which are in the western part of the park along the hills, comprise different species of *Brachystegia* woodland where sable and roan antelope occur.

The roads running along the Great Ruaha River and the northern section of the park along the Mwagusi Sand River are the two most popular areas of Ruaha with visitors making these the core areas. This is because of the all-weather roads, closeness of accommodation and because this is where most of Ruaha's wildlife is seen.

The road to the Msembe (turn right at R7) park headquarters has wonderful views across the river and the park towards the escarpment. The vegetation consists of light bush country composed mainly of species of *Combretum*, *Commiphora*, baobab and acacia. While there are several species of acacias along the river, the dominant tree in the area is *Faidherbia albida* (formerly known as *Acacia albida*).

Faidherbia albida, known in English as apple ring acacia, is one of the tallest trees reaching 30 m in height. It has a dense, rounded crown, rough and dull grey or brown bark, whitish branches and creamy coloured flowers which attract bees. Its most distinctive feature is the smooth bright orange seed pods which are curled and twisted like a corkscrew. Its leaves are retained in the dry season and fall in the rains.

This tree is an important component of the Ruaha ecosystem. It provides deep shade close to the river at the hottest times of the year, abundant fruit for animals, and the leaves provide increased nutrients for the soil during the wet season growth period. The roots bind the riverbanks reducing erosion and the resulting increased silt load in the river.

Elephants are attracted to the large groves of these trees for shade and fruit. But the resulting destruction leads to the groves shrinking. This in turn means less elephant visits and less regeneration of the shade-loving seeds of the *faidherbia albida*.

But the main reason for the tough times these trees and acacias have in regenerating is not the elephants and the array of seed-eating specialist insects which live in the shade. Any seed which manages to grow leaves becomes a prime target for dik-dik and impala with the result that few shooting trees make it to maturity.

Although the *faidherbia albida* groves are shrinking, the trees remain important to humans. The bark contains tannin which is used tanning, dying, the making of inks and medicines. The wood is used as timber including as handles for axes and hoes.

Acacia tortilis or the umbrella tree in English, offset by the sunset

Two roads lead from Msembe to Kimiramatonge Hill where you may also see klipspringer on the rocks as well as the rabbit-sized hyrax in colonies of 50 or more. There are also areas of grassland, thornbush, patches of forest and rocky hills.

The typical vegetation of the Mwagusi Sand River further north comprises tall stands of acacia and fig species, tamarind trees and clumps of towering duom palms, particularly around Mwagusi Safari Camp, as well as patches of open "black cotton soil" grassland and thickets where roads may become impassable during the rains.

This latter type of vegetation was previously often referred to as "thorn shrub" or "*nyika*". It is also the area where the visitor is most likely to see giraffe, plains game such as zebra, antelope and buffalo and carnivores such as lion, leopard and cheetah who prey upon them.

Elephant love the nuts of the duom palms

Beyond the valleys and to the north, the undulating terrain is dominated by baobabs scattered through scrubby *Combretum* and *Commiphora* woodland with occasional, distinct flat-topped acacia. In this area you are may find greater and lesser kudu, and groups of elephant.

The Lunda area, approached from Makuluga at the Mwagusi/Ruaha confluence, is not always passable during the rains as it crosses several *korongos* (dried deep river beds). There are palms lining the track as well as lots of baobab and regenerating acacia along the river. This area contains considerable grassland where various species including roan antelope and Grant's gazelle may be seen.

Mpululu is located on the escarpment 95 km from Mwagusi Sand River. During the rains it is advisable to check at park headquarters whether this road is passable as it goes through large areas of black cotton soil.

The road becomes more wooded as you climb the escarpment and the plateau has wonderful views of the park. The vegetation is mainly mixed *miombo* with *Combretum* and there are few animals in the dry season, most species remaining closer to water.

The road upstream (turn left at R7 after crossing bridge) along the Great Ruaha River leads past the Nyamakuyu Rapids which are only visible when the river is not in flood. This route meanders through grassland and then *Combretum* woodland and yet more baobab trees.

A male agama lizard

There are several species of *Combretum* in Ruaha National Park. These scraggy trees or shrubs are identifiable by their woody fruit which have four or five wings. *Combretum purpurifolia* stands out after the rains in the blur of green because of its scarlet tooth-brush flowers and pink five-flanged seed pods.

The flowers are eaten by many animals; kudu and giraffe love them as do insects (who number some three million in Africa and make up 70 percent of all species) and fruit-eating birds, many of whom acquire red faces in the process.

Ruaha is bounded by an escarpment above which *Brachystegia* and other typical woodland *miombo* species extend through the remainder of the park. Lichtenstein's hartebeest may be found in the drier area from Jongomeru to Magangwe although this is only a dry season track for 4x4 vehicles.

Further upstream the road leads on to Mkwawa and then past Trekimboga, a Wahehe word for the cooking of meat. The road follows the river closely and you may see various groups of animals such as waterbuck coming down to drink at midday and dusk here. In particular watch the termite mounds for mongoose.

Termites

You will see such mounds in many different parts of Ruaha. These are built by termites sometimes referred to as "white ants" although they are related to cockroaches. Like the earth worm of the northern hemisphere, the termites aerate the African soil.

The mounds vary in shape and size according to soil types and local climatic conditions and they incorporate a maze of complicated galleries and "fungus gardens" which provide food at regulated temperatures for the inhabitants.

As many as three million termites may live in a large mound. As in so much of the wild, the social order is strictly hierarchical and caste ridden. First comes the queen followed by the king, soldiers and workers, all inter-dependent, but each with a specific function.

During the rains, termites fly away seeking to establish new colonies. Few make it, the majority being eaten by humans and various other species.

The far southwest is characterised by evergreen upland/submontane forest dominated by *Drypetes gerrardii*. The forest is very inaccessible and whilst forest primates are known to exist, they have not been surveyed in detail.

Agama lizard can be readily seen along the Great Ruaha River. The male agama are spectacular with large, reddish-yellow heads, which they vigorously nod up and down, blue legs and hooded eyes. The female is dullish brown in colour.

One tree to look out for is the *Euphorbia ingens* which can be confused with the candelabra. This is an unmistakable savannah tree which grows to 15 m (49.5 feet) and has a crown of large ascending branches. The branches are soft and brittle producing a virulent sticky latex which is extremely toxic causing blindness in humans and blisters on the skin of cows.

The Mwagusi and Mdonya Sand Rivers are two of Ruaha's most magnificent features. Much of the year they are ribbons of sand, as their name suggests, concealing subterranean supplies of water interspersed with pools. The animal know about this hidden reservoir beneath the surface and elephant and baboon excavate the loose sand to obtain water.

During the rains the rivers become torrents feeding into the Great Ruaha River. The conversion by elephants of woodlands and bushlands to grasslands has made the area around Mbagi a good place for viewing buffalo who now have more grazing. The vegetation along the rivers can also conceal predators.

The road continues to Jongomeru where a new camp has been earmarked. This area is notable for its *Commiphora* woodlands and large groves of *Faidherbia albida*. If you are fortunate you may see leopard in the trees along the watercourse.

The drive along the river passes palm trees which are a feature of the valleys. The main one of these is *Hyphaene peterseon*. The other main species on the Mwayembe route are *Commiphora* found in the drier parts of Ruaha. This is readily recognisable by its twisted branches and peeling, papery bark.

Commiphora, in common with *Brachystegia* found on the escarpment, are leafless throughout most of the dry season. But they anticipate the rains with young, tender leaves appearing several weeks before the rains begin. This in turn may attract eland and other animals.

Miombo woodland consists mainly of *brachystegia* trees which, unlike acacia and allied trees elsewhere in Ruaha, are deciduous. They shed their broad leaves annually with new ones emerging just before the rains. The new leaves are usually red, russet or copper-coloured which attract birds such as the pale-billed hornbill.

Euphorbia ingens

ELEPHANTS

Ruaha National Park was notable for its heavily tusked elephants and it contains the largest elephant population found in any Tanzanian park. In the 1960s they numbered over 25,000. By 1990, elephant numbers in Ruaha (they were one of the major targets of the vast poaching scourge which was then sweeping southern Africa), had dropped to only 6,000. Today there are over 10,000 and that figure is steadily rising as evidenced by the considerable number of mothers with calves.

Disputed tusks

Early in the 1970s a police constable who was the driver of the Iringa regional police commander, was stopped at a roadblock and three pairs of tusks were found. The constable said he had shot the elephants with a borrowed rifle on a valid hunting licence while on his annual vacation.

The largest tusks weighed an astounding 203 and 199 lbs (101.5 and 99.5 kg), were 9 feet 3 inches and 8 feet 11 inches (3.1 to 2.7 m) in length and 26.5 inches (673 mm) at the tip.

They came from the biggest elephant shot in the 20th century. The largest tusks, also shot in Tanzania in 1899, are in the British Museum.

The constable was challenged to show the carcass of the elephant from which he said he had extracted the giant tusks. It was suspected the elephant had been shot in Ruaha National Park and expert evidence in a subsequent court case insisted that they could not have come from the carcass the constable identified. But the state lost the case.

The tusks, however, were confiscated by the state and when last seen were still in the ivory room in Dar es Salaam where, despite persistent rumours to the contrary, they had not been replaced by plastic replicas.

This celebrated court case coincided with the height of the poaching which swept the sub-continent. Rhinoceros used to reside in the park but none have been seen since 1982. The poachers tend to operate in the wet season when much of the park is cut off.

Opposite page: Male elephants are notable for their thicker, heavier tusks

Males carry larger tusks than females and for genetic reasons elephant in east Africa tend to have heavier ivory but smaller bodies than elephant found in southern Africa. The ivory tusks are elongated upper incisor teeth and as in the case of human teeth, the milk teeth are shed after about a year. Wear and tear causes the discrepancy in tusk sizes.

In the wild, elephant live to about 60 years of age and no mammal – other than humans – has the ability to change and disfigure their environment like the elephant does. Often heated debates result between the conservationists and those who would cull the elephants.

The origins of the African elephant (*Loxodonta africana*) are traced back 50 million years to their earliest ancestor, *Moeritherium*, a small pig-like creature whose fossil remains have been found on the swamp fringes of the Tethys Sea which covered the part of North Africa now known as the Sahara Desert.

Moeritherium was around 0.6 m at the shoulder and had no trunk. But its teeth and skull reveal it was the earliest known representative of five families of *proboscids,* an order to which the African elephant belongs.

Hyrax

As improbable as it may sound, the tiny hyrax, also known as a rock rabbit, you may see sunning itself on exposed rocks, is the closest living relative of the elephant.

The hyrax is about 500 mm in length and weighs three kg. Its body is covered by soft grizzled hair and it is tailless. At the centre of its back is a splash of yellow and the skins are sought after by humans as bedspreads. There are three species of hyrax, bush, rock and tree, and in Ruaha you are most likely to find bush or rock hyrax.

A hyrax

The woolly mammoth (*Mammuthus primigenius*), now extinct, is another earlier relative of the elephant. This species survived until humans established themselves on earth and its meat as once served in Leningrad by the Russian Tsar.

Woolly mammoth found in Siberia's permafrost in 1799. Its tusks were 4.8 metres (16 feet long), semi-circular and each weighed 125 kg (275 lbs)

The word elephant derives from the Greek word *"elphas"* which in Latin is *"elphantus"*. The word "pachyderms", to which they are scientifically referred, derives from their thick skins.

They are the most readily identifiable and unmistakable of African mammals. They have a gnarled appearance like a well-weathered tree, stand 3.5 m at the shoulder and weigh up to 6.5 tonnes.

But it is not just the enormous size and the ghost-like way they move that makes the elephant impressive. Almost every major structure in the elephant's body is specialised and their high levels of intelligence, complex behaviour and social structure makes them one of the most fascinating and studied animals in the bush.

In Ruaha there are two major aggregations of elephants. One is centred around the park headquarters at Msembe and the Mdonya River. The other is in the area of Mwagusi Sand River where one elephant named Constantine has become unusually friendly and wanders among the tents at Mwagusi Safari Camp.

The lack of nervousness of the Ruaha elephants, particularly bearing in mind the degree to which they were poached, is one of the most striking features about the park. So to is the number of tuskless and single tusk elephants, the reason for which presently falls within the realms of speculation.

The elephants creased skin is thickest on the legs (30 to 40 mm), forehead, trunk and back and thinnest on the ears. Until to age of 20 or 25, juvenile's bodies are covered with sparse bristly hair. Adults have distinctive eyelashes, green to hazel eyes and a tuft of hair at the end of their tails which are sought after as bracelets and were once used as pipe cleaners.

An elephant's skin colour is grey to brownish grey although this is not always discernible because of wallowing and dusting. Thick layers or cartilage on the feet act as shock-absorbers and the soles of the feet are horny and cracked. Frequently you will see an elephant standing on three legs as it temporarily raises and rests the fourth.

It is the trunk which holds the greatest fascination. Raised like a submarine periscope, it continuously probes the breeze checking for smell and danger such as lions. It is an extremely dextrous extension used for drinking and shovelling vast quantities of food into the small, spout shaped mouth with the elephant eating for three-quarters of the day.

The ear flaps are large reaching two metres in length in adult bulls. They weigh 20 kg each and constitute 20 percent of the body surface area. They have an extensive vascular system with the blood flow rate five to 12 litres per minute and they are vital to maintaining body temperature, emitting about three-quarters of total body heat loss. Experts recognise individual elephants by the nicks in their ears, and their tusks.

Checking the breeze for danger

Temperature control is important to all animals as well as humans. Elephant partially do this through continuously flapping their ears. Other methods include water intake (100 litres a day for mature animals), cooling through swimming and wallowing, and tossing water and dust over their bodies.

Elephant have temporal glands on either side of the head just above the eye. Males in musth (pronounced must) secrete from these glands leaving a dark stain down the face. This secretion is most copious when the animal is under stress or excited. Another sign that a male animal is in musth is the continuous dribbling of urine.

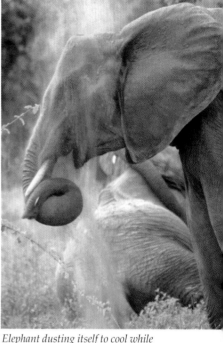

Elephant are catholic in their habitat requirements. Their range is wide and diverse *Elephant dusting itself to cool while another rolls nearby*

from the deserts of Namibia to the lusher zones of the tropics. They both graze and browse uprooting whole trees, tearing off large branches and they knock the soil off clumps of grass held in their trunks by banging the clumps on their feet or tusks.

In Ruaha the damage is not as conspicuous as that seen elsewhere on the continent: destroyed and damaged trees, bushes and branches on the tracks. Trees trunks are disfigured and worn by elephants rubbing on them. Attempts to topple trees, which elephant do with their rear feet planted firmly, tusks either side of the tree and trunks extended, may be seen. Elephant trails and cannonball-size droppings exist almost everywhere.

Water, preferably fresh, is a major requirement. Elephant travel 10 km or more a day in search of food and water. They smell water at considerable distances and they may charge towards it in whole herds or emerge silently from the tree line. After drinking, they retire to a salt lick if one exists.

Female elephant and young

Elephant dung is a breeding ground and sanctuary for many other smaller species. Foremost among these is the dung beetle, a member of the scarab family, which rolls the dung into balls and it pushes away using its back legs. The dung is then buried and the beetles lay eggs in it.

Elephants are gregarious living in family groups led by an adult female (matriach), her offspring and closely related females with their offspring. On reaching puberty at about 12 years old, young males leave of their own accord joining up with other young bulls. Family groups may coalesce into larger herds.

Mature bulls over the age of 30 will join the herds when a female is in oestrus. This oestrus lasts for only six days while the musth phase in bulls lasts for up to three months. Elephants are normally fairly peaceful animals. But a female in defence of her calves or a bull in musth can be very threatening.

An elephants raised head, with the trunk tucked below the jaw, ears extended, trumpeting and screaming may signal the real thing and not a mock charge and it is wise in these circumstances to beat a hasty retreat.

Sparring between young males is common but serious fights between adults rare. Elephants are deeply caring animals and if one dies, is shot or darted, the others in the herd are likely to protectively gather around and they may try to carry away the body of the inert animal, wedging it between their own bodies.

Conception occurs mainly during the rainy season with gestation taking 22 months. Females prefer shady and secluded places to give birth and the mother will normally be in a squatting position to lessen the calf's fall while severing the umbilical cord. The calves first reaction is to locate the two mammaries located between the mothers front legs and suckle.

Calves measure about 80 cm at the shoulder at birth. They are pinkish in colour

Spotting the difference between a mock charge and the real thing is not always easy

and their eyesight is very poor. They are weaned after about two years and until they are roughly 1.4 m at the shoulder they are threatened by predators, notably lion and hyena. As a result they stick close to their mothers and the herd will vigorously protect them from predators.

OTHER MAMMALS

One of the most compelling sights in Ruaha National Park is a pack of African hunting dogs. Ruaha is one of the few places in Africa where these elusive and enigmatic animals are still reasonably common and they are most frequently seen between Mwagusi Sand River and Jongomeru where the thick bush, however, may obscure sightings.

For nine months of the year they hunt covering hundreds of sq km at their fast loping pace. The remainder of the year is spent close to their den where a new litter is born and cared for lovingly by the pack.

African hunting dog

The first time I ever saw these animals they were then known as "wild" dogs. I had been given a lift in the 1960s to the Selous Game Reserve in southern Tanzania by a European hunter when we chanced on a pack of what I was to learn were African hunting dogs.

The hunter immediately stopped his vehicle and he and his gun-bearer grabbed their guns, leapt out and started shooting the animals. When I protested I was told they were "vermin" who killed domestic livestock and drove wild animals out of areas where they resided.

That incident is indelibly etched on my memory like a terrifying nightmare. Forty-years on I still wonder how anybody - and this was official policy throughout Africa (Southern Rhodesian farmers recorded shooting 2,674 in the five years up to 1961) - could regard this beautifully marked animal as "vermin" and put a price on its head "dead only".

Scientifically the African hunting dog is known as *Lycaon pictus* which literally translates as painted wolf.

They have large, rounded ears and their coats are blotched mustard, white and black with white-tipped tails.

They are very social animals living in packs of six to 20. Each pack consists of a dominant breeding pair, their offspring and the dominant male's brothers. Young females migrate joining other packs and suffer high mortality.

Opposite page: African hunting dogs

Gestation lasts for approximately 70 days and the dominant female will excavate several holes before choosing one to give birth. An average of 10 pups are born in each litter and they are hidden for months with other dogs in the pack feeding the mother, who rarely joins hunts. Noisy begging for food by the mother and her puppies indicates the hunters' return.

Lactation is brief and the puppies are swiftly weaned and fed on meat regurgitated by the mother. The puppies are very vulnerable to predators in this phase and an adult may remain on guard while the rest of the pack hunts. A gruff bark signals danger and sends the litter scurrying for the safety of the den.

A well marked female carrying pups

The sharing of food and other duties is an essential part of the hunting dogs life and an illustration of the cohesive nature of their society. At about three months, when the puppies are ready to leave their den, they are taught to hunt. But, until they are about a year old, they depend upon adults for food and are given precedence at kills.

They are very social animals greeting each other with much tail-wagging, playing and general bedlam. They hunt together chasing down their preferred prey of small antelope or the calves or larger animals at speeds of up to 60 kph. The kills can be gruesome and may occur within metres of people. They are very prone to domestic canine from which they have no immunity.

On average the hunting dog lives until ten years old. Disease, flooded dens, other predators and humans, particularly motorists and farmers, cause a high mortality rate. There are no cases of these animals becoming domesticated and equally there are no verified cases of them attacking humans.

Another of Ruaha's many compelling animals is the greater kudu (*Tragelaphus strepsiceros*). These animals are most likely to be seen in dense bush country. The horns of the males, long prized in Africa as musical instruments, honey containers and as ritual objects, are spectacularly spiralled and may grow to 180 cm in length in a series of graceful twists.

The horns are rarely used in fights among kudu or in defence against predators. In wooded country the kudu tilts its chin skywards and lays its horns along its back to avoid them becoming entangled in thickets.

Both greater and lesser kudu (*Tragelaphus imberbis*) exist in Ruaha. Both have stripes and spots on their bodies and a "v" shaped chevron of white hair on the forehead between the eyes. A crest of long hair runs down the spine and some kudu have a distinct fringe of hair on the underside of the neck. Their cryptic colouring blends in with the bush making them difficult to see, particularly because when alarmed they stand very still.

Female greater kudu

Telling greater and lesser kudu apart is difficult for the untrained eye. Size is one way. The lesser kudu also has smaller horns, two conspicuous white patches on the upper and lower portion of the neck and about six more lateral stripes than the greater kudu giving a total of 11 to 15.

Usually only the male kudu are horned. Females are found in groups of six to ten animals, including their young. They walk hesitantly yet elegantly, particularly when approaching water. Males, except during mating, are solitary or found in bachelor herds.

Near the park headquarters, usually amidst acacia groves, you may see a herd of rusty-grey antelope who canter away, then stop and turn to watch you. If they have large fringed ears, black and white facial markings, then they are roan (*Hippotragus equinus*) antelope who weigh between 220 and 270 kg.

Both female and male roan antelope carry boldly ridged, backward sweeping horns although those on the bulls are considerably thicker and more curved. They are principally grazers feeding on leaves. But they will browse on tender twigs and they drink regularly, usually in the mornings.

Sable (*Hippotragus niger*), who are closely related to and resemble the larger roan, may be seen in miombo woodland on the road to Mpululu starting at Mwagusi Sand River. They are magnificent animals with

males having glossy black and females chestnut-brown coats. Young are born paler developing adult colouration with age.

Both the female and the male sable have scimitar-shaped horns which sweep backwards in a graceful curve. They are found in groups of females with young, all-male bachelor herds and solitary males occupying territory. Males only mate with a female who transacts his territory and they will allow subordinate males into the area as long as they show no interest in the females. But they will defend their territory against other dominant males.

Sable

The fourth large antelope you may see at Ruaha is the eland (*Taurotragus oryx*). This is the largest antelope weighing 800 kg. The biggest herd of them was in Russia's Ural Mountains where they were bred by a former Tsar because of the low cholesterol content of their meat and milk which were used in the treatment of patients with heart ailments.

Eland are versatile animals who move around a great deal, particularly during the dry season, and it is therefore difficult to pinpoint where they are most likely to be seen at Ruaha. They occur on the fringes of, but do not penetrate, forests and they generally avoid more extensive, open grass plains except in transit.

They are predominantly browsers who require small trees or bushes to provide this part of their diet. Farmers have used them alongside domestic cattle (grazers) to control tsetse fly in cleared bush areas by combining these two species eating habits.

When water is available, eland will drink regularly although they obtain the moisture they require from their food and proximity to water is not a habitat requirement as it is with many other species.

There are nine other species of antelope you may see in Ruaha. These include Lichenstein's hartebeest (*Alecelaphus lichtensteinii*) which is reddish-fawn in colour, has a long face and short, ridged horns with their tips pointing backwards. These animals are often referred to as *"kongoni"* which is the Swahili word for the species.

Kongoni or hartebeest

Grant's gazelle (*Gazella granti*), which are on the southern limit of their distribution range, may also be seen on River Drive. They are large, pale fawn-coloured animals with long legs. Males are larger and heavier than females with longer horns. The horns are very stout at the base curving evenly backwards in a harp shape, ending with a slight curve forwards.

The white patch on the rump and sharply contrasting stripe down the thigh is very conspicuous on the Grant's and the female has black skin around her teats which are thought to visually make the source of milk more recognisable to the ewes.

Gazelle are specially fond of open grass plains and are both grazers and browsers, their diet being dictated by the season. They are gregarious animals who are not water dependent and their large salivary glands secrete fluid into their relatively dry diet.

In contrast Defassa waterbuck (*Kobus defassa*) inhabits areas close to water and are found grazing on savannah grasslands, on forest edges and in riverine woodlands. Mainly grazers, they eat coarse grasses. This is a thickset antelope with a shaggy, brownish-grey coat with ringed, forward sweeping horns on the male. They have a distinct goat-like aroma.

Waterbuck

Dik-dik

Kirk's dik-dik *(Rhynchotragus kirki)* are a drab grey in colour, weigh only about four kg with the female somewhat heavier than the male, have large luminous eyes and pointed noses, and they literally spring up underfoot or zigzag singly or in pairs away from vehicles before disappearing into the bush.

Bushbuck *(Tragelaphus scriptus)* are secretive medium-sized animals with rufous-brown coats (darker in older males) and light spots on the haunches giving them a bambi-like appearance. Both males and females have geometrically shaped patches on the ears, chin, tail, legs and neck, vertical stripes on the body and half collars at the base of the neck.

Bohor reedbuck *(Redunca redunca)* have been seen on the road to Mpulu. Easily confused with impala, they are uniformly sandy-red in colour and the males have short, forward thrusting horns. They emit a shrill whistle when alarmed and disappear with a rocking horse gait.

Klipspringer

Klipspringer *(Oreotragus oreotragus)* are often visible on the rocks. They are grey, thick-set and rough coated and they jump from one rock to another on their narrow, almost cylindrical hooves rather like goats. Their balance is effortless and they are usually seen in pairs or with one smaller offspring. The Klipspringer you will see at Ruaha are from the Maasai race with both the male and female having horns.

Lion in Ruaha, because of the wide distribution of their preferred prey species and the nature of the country, cannot afford to lie around as much as their more numerous cousins do in the Serengeti and Ngorongoro. Lion will be found where their prey, including buffalo, zebra and antelope, exists.

Despite this, lion activity is mainly nocturnal and if you happen upon them during the day they will most likely be resting preparing for the nights hunt or licking, grooming, playing and greeting each other like very large domestic cats. The rubbing of heads and whole bodies is their recognisable form of greeting each other.

They live in groups known as prides with a large territorial range. These may include five to ten related mothers, daughters, sisters, cousins and aunts and the cubs may suckle from any lactating female so that if the mother dies the other females in the pride raise the orphan.

Male lions are quite different. There are usually two or three in a pride who mark,

Young male lion, his mane not yet black

patrol and defend the territory. Within this range one or two lioness may live. Sometimes the lion will kill unrelated cubs so that their direct progeny are unchallenged.

Lions hunt at night with the lioness doing 85 to 90 percent of the hunting. Nevertheless the male usually eats first. Lions hunt, not always successfully, by stalking their intended prey in a crouched position. Then they rush the victim stunning it with a powerful blow from the massive paws and legs or throttling it with their powerful jaws. They will often drag the carcass into the shade.

Leopards are widespread in Ruaha. But they are elusive and secretive animals and their kill may be seen in the fork of a tree, where it has been stored out of the way of lion and hyena.

The road leading south along the Great Ruaha River towards Jongomeru is one of the places where you may see this beautiful animal with its irregular rosette spots on their yellowish-grey coats and white underparts. On the back of each ear there is a distinct white spot and the tail is long and spotted.

Leopard

Leopards are solitary animals except during mating. Females with cubs can be very aggressive. They are stealthy stalkers of their prey with a far higher kill ratio than lion. They vocalise through a repeated rasping or sawing cough and do not roar like lions.

The cheetah is an elegant plains animal which is well camouflaged in dry grass. Sometimes mistaken for a leopard, it is much lighter in build, has spots (as opposed to the leopards' rosettes) on its body, "tear" marks from the eyes to mouth and its is the fastest animal on earth with its speed exceeding 100 kph in brief bursts when hunting.

They are specialised predators who rely on a concealed approach to their intended victim followed by a short chase of no more than 300 metres because their bodies rapidly overheat. Unlike lion, they mainly hunt during daylight hours relying upon their eyesight. In Ruaha their diet consists mainly of dikdik, impala, young warthog, hares and birds.

Serval, which look like miniature leopard, are almost entirely nocturnal and their diet consists of game birds, snakes, lizards, frogs and insects. Their large ears and acute hearing helps them to locate potential prey. Once a sound is located, they approach stealthily, leaping and pouncing on the victim.

The black-backed jackal is a small carnivore with a silver-streaked black saddle, and yellowish-rust covered flanks and legs. It has a dog-like appearance and while primarily a scavenger it will kills for itself with the prey ranging from baby antelope to dung beetles.

Jackals are usually found in pairs and they are one of the few species of mammals that mate for life. When pups are born, the mothers stays in the den with the litter while the father feeds the family. Within six months the cubs hunt on their own and they may stay with their parents to help raise future generations, to guard and to baby-sit the pups as well as to regurgitate the food when the mother is in lactation.

Two species of hyena, spotted and striped, occur in Ruaha. They have sloping backs, short broad muzzles and rounded ears in the case of spotted hyena (*Crocuta crocuta*). They live in clans of related relatives which may number up to 100 and they are skilful hunters as well as scavengers. A pack pulls down its prey and devours it in minutes with the powerful jaws and digestive tract obtaining nutrients even from the skin and bone.

Spotted Hyena

Apart from their pointed ears, the striped hyena (*Hyaena hyaena*) is identifiable by its grey body markings including black vertical stripes, a shaggy mane and bushy tail as well as its noticeably lesser size.

Buffalo (*Syncerus caffer*) are numerous throughout the park and one explanation advanced for their increasing numbers is that elephant damage has transformed former woodland and forest areas into open grasslands where the buffalo can graze and feel more secure.

Male Buffalo

A mature adult male buffalo can weigh up to 800 kg. They measure one-and-a-half m at the shoulder which carries the massive head and horns. The male's formidable horns are joined by a bony protuberance (known as a boss) with which they pound their victim.

They are primarily grazers who feed more at night than by day. In the day you may see egrets ahead of them waiting for them to kick up grasshoppers and other insects and red (more common in Ruaha and distinguished by their yellow eye-ring) and yellow-billed oxpeckers known as tickbirds feeding from the parasites on their bodies.

Buffalo must drink regularly and will usually be found near water. A good place to see them is around Mbagi in the north of the park on the Mwagusi Sand River. They may be seen in bachelor herds, as single old bulls, or in vast breeding herds numbering hundreds of females, calves and several adult males.

Giraffe (*Giraffa camelopardalis*) are also likely to be seen browsing on acacia trees and other bush species in the Mwagusi Sand River area. With their puckered mouths and long tongues, they eat the shoots and other edible portions of acacia while carefully avoiding the thorns.

Like humans, they have seven vertebrae even though male giraffe reach five m (16.5 feet) in height. Females are about a m shorter and lighter in colour. A male weighs 800 to 1,000 kg and giraffe (those in Ruaha are the Maasai species) have irregular star-shaped markings over most of their bodies.

Males, who have a strong dominance hierarchy and who spar standing shoulder to shoulder and entwining their long necks (this is called "necking") are distinguishable from females by their sturdier "horns" which are in fact thickened bone covered by skin. Female "horns" are thinner and often hair-tufted.

One characteristic of the giraffe is its gait, making it a drill sergeant's nightmare. When they are walking, both limbs on the same side swing forward together, and when they are galloping the two hind legs swing forward together followed by the forelegs.

Zebra, oblivious to the elephant, watches the photographer

No two zebra (*Equus crawshayi*), it is frequently said, are alike. The same statement could be applied to any other mammal, including humans, for even in rare cases of identical twins they are not exactly alike. Lions are told apart by the spots on their faces, elephants by the tears in their ears and so on.

The stripe pattern, including the shadows, is different on every zebra. In daylight their black and white stripes are conspicuous. But by night, or in a heat haze, their colouration blends into their surroundings making them harder to see.

They live in family groups headed by a dominant stallion, several females, subordinate males and juveniles. Each group has a dominant female who leads the group in single file with each mares respective foal trailing behind her.

Warthog, whom you are most likely to see in family groups running away from you with their hair-tipped tails erect like antennae, have been variously described as "incarnations of hideous dreams" and "the most astonishing objects that have ever disgraced nature".

Warthog with tail erect, hurries away

That is a harsh judgement of this captivating animal. The males have impressively curved tusks which they use as protection, even taking on lion. They live in family groups with the young entering burrows head first and the parents backwards to fight off threatening predators. When grazing they may kneel on their calloused forelegs to eat.

Stockily built, the warthog has a short neck and a long tapering head ending in a blunt, rounded snout giving it a pig-like appearance. The body has sparse, bristly hair and the male has four prominent facial warts against two on the female.

The name for the hippopotamus (*Hippopotamus amphibius*) is an English colloquial name derived from the Greek word for a water or river horse. They weigh two to three tonnes, are four metres in length, and they have a stocky rounded body set on top of stumpy legs.

They spend most of the day submerged in water and the easiest place to see hippopotamus is close to the Great Ruaha River bridge down a track to the Hippo Pool.

Hippopotamus have a porous skin which prevents dehydration. They can stay underwater for six minutes returning noisily to the surface where they immediately exhale. The calves can suckle under water. They grunt continually and scatter their dung with their stumpy tails rather as a farm muck-spreader distributes its load.

From the safety of the bank they appear placid. But males fight viciously over territory and they can be aggressive towards humans in boats and those on foot who are foolhardy enough to get between them and water.

Hippopotamus changing pools in the remnants of the Great Ruaha River

Nightly, using defined trails, they leave the water to graze. Often they roam considerable distances eating up to 50 kg of food, mainly grasses and sedges. The oldest and strongest males usually dominate the social hierarchy and even in water they can be told apart from the females by their larger necks and upright ears. Individuals can be identified by their wrinkle pattern, a pursuit which should only be attempted with binoculars.

Porcupine (*Hystrix cristata*), ratel or honeybadger (*Mellivora capensis*), aardwolf (*Proteles cristatus*), bat-eared fox (*Otocyon megalotis*) and five species of mongoose, the most common of which are banded (*Mungos mungo*), dwarf (*Helogale undulata*) and slender (*Herpestes sanguineus*) may also be seen.

Yellow baboon (*Papio cynocephalus*) at Ruaha are lighter in colour and build than the olive baboon in northern Tanzania. Their diet comprises of grass, fruit and insects but they also kill young antelopes. They make over 30 noises ranging through grunts, barks and screams and often they will signal the presence of leopard.

Yellow baboon (left) on top of a junction sign is unphased by the male impala bounding over him and a bat-eared fox (right) rarely seen in daylight

Their major requirements are food, water and shelter which means tall trees or rock faces to sleep safely. Troops of baboons may number over 100 and they are cohesive units where the young, black babies are transported on their mothers' backs.

In contrast, vervet monkeys (*Cercopithecus aethiops*) are much smaller with black faces, white cheek tufts and grey fur. They eat insects, fruit, leaves, seeds, young birds, eggs and anything humans leave lying around. They twitter to warn each other of impending danger and rapidly retreat if threatened.

The final large species you will see at Ruaha is a reptile and not a mammal. Nile crocodiles (*Crocodilus nilotica*) are primitive in appearance and crocodiles are the sole surviving descendants of one of the most successful groups of land-dwelling vertebrates, the *Archosauria* or ruling reptiles.

During the Mesozoic era 65 to 245 million years ago in the age of dinosaurs, these reptiles dominated the animal communities. Despite their antiquity, it is inappropriate to treat crocodiles as "living fossils" limited to a marginal role for they have undergone considerable change during their 200 million years of evolution.

BIRDS

A total of 436 bird species have so far been identified in Ruaha but some habitat types are poorly covered and the list continues to grow. The total will probably stabilize at around 475 species, much the same as France or California.

Because the Great Ruaha River dominates the park, the waterbirds are concentrated on here. Then come the larger and more conspicuous species. Many species of game birds, dove, lovebirds, bee-eater, barbet, honeyguide, swallow, martin, thrush, shrike, starling, sunbird, sparrow, weaver, waxbill, whydah and bunting are also evident.

Although Ruaha is one of the driest parts of Tanzania, the river and seasonal swamps attract a wide variety of waterbirds. Both pink-backed and white pelicans form large feeding flocks when the river dries and fish concentrate in the remaining pools.

Goliath herons, great white egrets, saddle-billed storks and yellow-billed storks are the resident large waterbirds along the river. Of particular interest to birdwatchers is the population of the rare and secretive white-backed night herons which roosts by day in the dense foliage along the river.

Black-faced sand grouse

The iridescent open-billed stork (the gap between the closed bill enables it to grasp large round water snails), is more of a seasonal visitor breeding beyond the park boundary. When the December rains are heavy, Ruaha often attracts large numbers of migrant white and Abdim's stork. They feed on explosions of grasshoppers and army worms moving on when infestations are depleted.

Ducks and geese are generally not well represented in Ruaha but the river holds large numbers of Egyptian geese which form flocks after the breeding season when the birds become flightless during their annual moult.

During the European winter the river is frequented by a wide variety of wading birds, their numbers are usually low because the available habitat is limited but the variety is excellent. So, if you are really into your birds, check out these waders and perhaps you'll have the chance to add a species or two to the park list.

Opposite page: Lilac-breasted roller

However, the dominant wader along the river is the white-headed plover. This species is confined to these large rivers, a breeding habitat it shares with the African skimmer, a most amazing relative of the nominally sea-going family of terns. The lower part of the long red bill is longer than the upper and it feeds by skimming low over the water with its bill tip tracing the surface.

With many of the larger game animals disappearing from unprotected land, the vultures and other birds of prey that rely on them as a source of food are also becoming concentrated within National Parks and Game Reserves.

There are six species of vultures in Ruaha, all of which may be seen during a single visit. The most common is the brown, white-backed vulture which dominates at carcasses even though it is smaller than the rarer lappet-faced and Ruppell's vultures.

Among the smaller eagles the African hawk eagle is reasonably common in Ruaha, and the acrobat in the sky, the bateleur, will be seen throughout the day. Its short tail gives it a distinctive silhouette as it rides the air currents on rigid wings, rarely needing to flap once the heat is rising from the land.

The martial eagle, the largest bird of prey in Africa is usually seen and the migrant Whalberg's eagle arrives to breed towards the end of August from wintering grounds north of the equator.

Among the smaller raptors, Ruaha is noted for its wintering population of sooty falcons, migrants from the edge of the great Sahara Desert, and the even

Weaver nests

rarer Eleonora's falcon which breeds along the sea cliffs of the Mediterranean Sea. The smaller red-necked falcon is resident and more or less confined to river valleys dominated by borassus palms, its preferred nest site.

Silvery-cheeked hornbill

It is perhaps the hornbills that will leave the most lasting memory for they occur throughout the park. The less common of the six species is the pale-billed hornbill which is more or less confined to miombo woodland. Its nearest relative is the grey hornbill, a common and widespread species within dry woodland habitats.

Perhaps the two most often seen species are the red-billed and Von der Decken's hornbill. Both have red bills but the former has a longer, thinner and more pointed bill with white spots on its wing coverts which are lacking in Von der Decken's. The female Von der Decken's has an all black bill.

All hornbills nest in cavities where they wall in the female with mud, leaving only a narrow slit through which the male must feed her while she incubates and broods the young. During this period she becomes flightless, moulting all her wing and tail feathers.

When the young have sufficient feathers to maintain their body temperature, the female breaks out of the nest and joins the male in feeding the young through a freshly built, mud wall.

Of all the hornbills, the most fascinating is also the largest. Ground hornbills are becoming scarcer throughout their wide African range, perhaps because as agriculture intensifies there are fewer large prey items and fewer suitable nest sites. Family parties are often seen in Ruaha, stalking the ground in their search for any prey small enough to be swallowed whole.

Red-billed hornbill

From frogs and insects to small birds and the occasional fallen fruit, these omnivorous birds are formidable eating machines. The bright red facial skin of the adults is set against an almost black body colouring and they have the most stunning pair of eyelashes.

Tanzania National Parks (TANAPA) initial conservation mandate had been spelt out in September 1961 on the eve of independence at a symposium on Conservation of Nature and Natural Resources by the country's late founding president, Julius Nyerere. His words then are worth remembering for they were an important part of TANAPA's evolution.

The Arusha Manifesto

"The survival of our wildlife is a matter of grave concern to all of us in Africa. These wild creatures amid the wild places they inhabit are not only important as a source of wonder and inspiration but are an integral part of our natural resources and our future livelihood and well being.

"In accepting the trusteeship of our wildlife we solemnly declare that we will do everything in our power to make sure that our children's grandchildren will be able to enjoy this rich and precious inheritance.

"The conservation of wildlife and wild places calls for specialist knowledge, trained manpower, and money, and we look to other nations to cooperate with us in this important task - the success or failure of which not only affects the continent of Africa but the rest of the world as well."

At independence in December 1961, Tanganyika (as the mainland was then known before the union with Zanzibar), had only one national park, the internationally acclaimed Serengeti. Today the number is 12 with new ones and extensions to existing parks under active debate.

Parks cover 4.5 percent of Tanzania's land area and to this should be added 30 game reserves, 48 game controlled areas and 535 forest reserves making the total area of the country devoted to conservation 20 percent of the 945,188 sq km (364,943 sq miles) total.

In 1988, as conservation thinking evolved, the Community Conservation Services (CCS) was created as a wing of TANAPA with a pilot scheme in the Serengeti. The new organisation seeks to share park benefits and reduce conflicts with neighbouring communities.

Today Tanzania's infrastructure is rapidly improving and in the view of most regional experts the country has become Africa's number one safari destination.

PARK REGULATIONS

TANAPA's is a government parastatal headquartered in Arusha. It is responsible for gazetting, management and protection of the country's 12 national parks at Arusha, Gombe Stream, Katavi, Kilimanjaro, Lake Manyara, Mahale Mountains, Mikumi, Ruaha, Rubondo Island, Serengeti, Tarangire and Udzungwa. The following park regulations, some of which apply to specific parks, are published for visitors' guidance. Do not:

● Disturb any animals or birds;

● Cause any noise or create a disturbance likely to offend or annoy other visitors;

● Pick any flowers or cut or destroy any vegetation;

● Discard any litter, burning cigarettes or matches;

● Bring a pet into the park;

● Bring a firearm into the park.

● Feed any of the animals;

● Enter the park without an official guide;

● Take children below the age of seven into the park;

● Stray from the main trails;

In addition to these regulations which apply to all Tanzania National Parks, there are some special regulations for Gombe Stream and Mahale Mountains. These are:

● Keep at least five metres (15 feet) from the primates at all times.

● If a male chimpanzee charges you, move quickly to a tree and hold on tightly. The chances are that he will not hurt you if you do this;

● Respect those chimpanzees who seem to be shy. Do not follow them if they seem to be avoiding you. Never come between a mother and her child.

Ruaha National Park is 130 km from the regional capital of Iringa in southcentral Tanzania. The drive from Iringa takes about two-and-a-half hours. The entrance gate is nine km from the park boundary and the park headquarters are a further nine km on at Msembe.

Ruaha NP has one landing strip at Msembe. The flight from Dar es Salaam to Msembe takes about two-and-a-half hours in a light aircraft. Ground transport should be arranged in advance so you are met and transport can be rented through Ruaha River Lodge. The nearest fuel for sale is in Iringa and campers should be fully self-contained.

The campsites are on the banks of the Ruaha River at Msembe. They have pit latrines but no water. This is available for drinking and showering at the nearby *bandas* (huts). The hostel, used by groups visiting the park, sleeps 32 people. Mattresses and kitchen facilities are provided but visitors must have their own transport.

Bookings for *bandas*, campsites and the hostel must be made through the chief park warden whose address is Ruaha National Park, PO Box 369, Iringa, Tanzania. There is a small dispensary at the park headquarters where first aid can be administered.

Ruaha River Lodge. Box 10270, Dar es Salaam. Tel/fax: 255 (0)811.327706. E-mail: <fox@twiga.com>. Web: <www.ruahariverlodge.com>. Accommodation at the three lodges (original, *kopje* and river) is comfortable and located on the banks of the Great Ruaha River where hippopotamus nosily cavort. The *kopje* bar has panoramic views of the river below and the *kopje* and downstream river camp both have restaurants where you can watch the animals coming down to drink.

Mwagusi Safari Camp. Bookings through <tropicafrica.uk@virgin.net> or <davidmoyer@maf.org> marked attention Magusi Safari Camp. This is authentic Africa at its finest. Christopher Fox cares passionately about the bush where he was raised and his 16-bed camp, its rustic yet basic comfort and the surprising number of animals in the area throughout the year, reveals his deep affinity with nature and its many facets.

Precision Air. Box 1636, Arusha, Tanzania. Tel: 6903, 2818, 7319. Fax: 8204. Telex: 42148/50008. Mobile: (0811) 888644. E-mail: <precision-ark@cybernet.co.tz>. This private airline flies to Iringa and on to Mbeya twice a week. It also has flights to Dar es Salaam, Zanzibar, Arusha and other Tanzanian internal destinations and to Kenya.

CHECKLISTS

MAMMALS

English	Swahili/Vernacular	Latin
Aardwolf	*Fisi Mdogo*	*Proteles christatus*
Antelope, Roan	*Korongo*	*Hippotragus equinus*
Antelope, Sable	*Pala hala or Mbarapi*	*Hippotragus niger*
Baboon, yellow	*Nyani*	*Papio cynocephalus*
Buffalo	*Nyati or Mbogo*	*Syncerus caffer*
Bushbuck	*Pongo*	*Tragelaphus scriptus*
Cheetah	*Duma*	*Acinonyx jubatus*
Dikdik, Kirks	*Digidigi or Saruya*	*Rhynchotragus kirki*
Dog, African hunting	*Mbwa mwitu*	*Lycaon pictus*
Eland, Livingstone's	*Pofu*	*Taurotragus oryx*
Elephant, African	*Tembo or Ndovu*	*Loxodonta africana*
Fox, bat-eared	*Mbweha masikio*	*Otocyon megalotis*
Gazelle, Grant's	*Swala granti*	*Gazella granti*
Giraffe, Maasai	*Twiga*	*Giraffa camelopardalis*
Hartebeest, Lichenstein's	*Kongoni*	*Alecelaphus lichtensteinii*
Hippopotamus	*Kiboko*	*Hippotopamus amphibius*
Hyena, spotted	*Fisi*	*Crocuta crocuta*
Hyena, striped	*Fisi*	*Hyaena hyaena*
Hyrax, rock	*Pimbi*	*Procavia johnstoni*
Impala	*Swala pala*	*Aepyceros melampus*
Jackal, black-backed	*Mbweha shaba or mweusi*	*Canis mesomelas*
Klipspringer	*Mbuzi mawe*	*Oreotragus oreotragus*
Kudu, greater	*Tandala Mkubwa*	*Tragelaphus strepsiceros*
Kudu, lesser	*Tandala ndogo*	*Tragelaphus imberbis*
Leopard	*Chui*	*Panthera pardus*
Lion	*Simba*	*Panthera leo*
Mongoose, banded	*Kicheche*	*Mungos mungo*
Mongoose, dwarf	*Kicheche*	*Helogale undulata*
Mongoose, slender	*Kicheche*	*Herpestes sanguineus*
Monkey, vervet	*Tumbili*	*Cercopithecus aethiops*
Porcupine, crested	*Nungunungu*	*Hystrix crisdata*
Ratel (Honey badger)	*Nyegere*	*Mellivora capensis*
Reedbuck, Bohor	*Tohe*	*Redunca redunca*
Serval	*Mondo or kisongo*	*Felis serval*
Steinbuck	*Tondoro*	*Raphicerus campestris*
Warthog	*Ngiri*	*Phacochoerus aethiopicus*
Waterbuck, Defassa	*Kuro*	*Kobus defassa*
Zebra, Burchell's	*Punda milia*	*Equus burchelli*

BIRDS: ~~A complete list of Ruaha birds has been compiled by Rob Glen~~ and is for sale at the park. This list is therefore abridged.

English name

Ostrich
Pink-backed pelican
Darter
Dwarf bittern
Goliath heron
Rufous-bellied heron
Green-backed heron
White-backed night heron
Abdim's stork
White stork
Woolly-necked stork
Black stork
Saddle-billed stork
Egyptian goose
Secretary bird
Ruppell's griffon vulture
Lappet-faced vulture
White-headed vulture
Pallid harrier
Montagu's harrier
African marsh harrier
Harrier hawk
Western banded snake eagle
Bateleur
Ovampo sparrowhawk
Steppe eagle
Lesser-spotted eagle
Tawny eagle
Verreaux's eagle
Wahlberg's eagle
Grasshopper buzzard
Augur buzzard
Ayres' hawk eagle
African hawk eagle
Long-crested eagle
Gabar goshawk
Pale chanting goshawk
Martial eagle
Crowned eagle
Black-shouldered kite
Eastern red-footed falcon
Grey kestrel
Lanner falcon

Red-necked falcon
Hobby
Pygmy falcon
Harlequin quail
Coqui francolin
Hildebrandt's francolin
Crested francolin
Helmeted francolin
Crested guineafowl
Button quail
Crowned crane
African crane
Lesser moorhen
Common moorhen
African finfoot
Black-bellied bustard
White-bellied bustard
Denham's bustard
Painted snipe
Ringed plover
Three-banded sandplover
White-headed plover
Senegal plover
Wattled plover
Wood sandpiper
Greenshank
Marsh sandpiper
Common snipe
Little stilt
Black-winged stilt
Avocet
Spotted thicknee
Water thicknee
Temminck's courser
Violet-tipped courser
Heuglin's courser
Common pratincole
Lesser crested tern
African skimmer
Black-faced sandgrouse
Yellow-throated sandgrouse
Speckled pigeon
Emerald-spotted wood dove
Green pigeon
Yellow-collared lovebird

Brown parrot
Brown-necked parrot
Bare-faced go-away bird
Violet-crested turaco
Emerald cuckoo
Klaas'cuckoo
Great spotted cuckoo
Black and white cuckoo
Levaillant's cuckoo
African cuckoo
Red-chested cuckoo
Black coucal
Senegal coucal
Barn owl
Verreaux's eagle owl
Pearl-spotted owlet
African scops owl
Pel's fishing owl
Eurasian nightjar
Freckled nightjar
Pennant-winged nightjar
Mottled swift
White-rumped swift
Alpine swift
Palm swift
Boehm's spinetail
Mottle-throated spinetail
Blue-naped mousebird
Narina's trogon
Giant kingfisher
Half-collared kingfisher
Brown-hooded kingfisher
Woodland kingfisher
Pygmy kingfisher
Swallow-tailed bee-eater
Carmine bee-eater
Blue-cheeked bee-eater
Madagascar bee-eater
Lilac-breasted roller
Eurasian roller
Rufous-crowned roller
Racquet-tailed roller
Broad-billed roller
Abyssinian scimitarbill
Trumpeter hornbill
Crowned hornbill
Red-billed hornbill
Grey hornbill

Pale-billed hornbill
Ground hornbill
Spotted-flanked barbet
Black-collared barbet
Red-fronted tinkerbird
Red and yellow barbet
Levaillant's barbet
Black-throated honeyguide
Lesser honeyguide
Wahlberg's honeybird
Golden-tailed woodpecker
Little-spotted woodpecker
Nubian woodpecker
Bearded woodpecker
Red-capped lark
Dusky-bush lark
Flappet lark
House martin
Angola swallow
African rock martin
Grey-rumped swallow
Mosque swallow
White-haired roughwing
Black roughwing
Banded martin
African sand martin
African golden oriole
Black-headed oriole
Golden oriole
White-necked raven
White-bellied tit
African penduline tit
Spotted creeper
Scaly chatterer
Black-lored babbler
Black cuckoo shrike
White-breasted cuckoo shrike
Yellow-bellied greenbull
White-browed shrub robin
Morning thrush
Spotted morning thrush
White-browed robin chat
Red-capped robin chat
Irania
Sprosser
Nightingale
Rock thrush
Isabelline wheatear

Northern wheatear
Capped wheatear
White-headed black chat
Cliff chat
Kurrichane thrush
Groundscraper thrush
Grey wren warbler
Desert cisticola
Rattling cisticola
Tabora cisticola
Zitting cisticola
Croaking cisticola
Yellow-bellied eremomela
Green-capped eremomela
Icterine warbler
Upcher's warbler
Olivaceous warbler
Garden warbler
Whitethroat
Red-faced crombec
Grey flycatcher
Collared flycatcher
Southern black flycatcher
Ashy flycatcher
Lead-coloured flycatcher
Chin-spot batis
Yellow-throated longclaw
White wagtail
Mountain wagtail
Yellow wagtail
Golden pipit
Slate-coloured boubou
Grey-headed bush shrike
Sulphur-breasted bush shrike
Brubru
Marsh tchagra
Magpie shrike
Long-tailed fiscal
Red-backed shrike
Red-tailed shrike
Retz's shrike
Ashy starling
Blue-eared starling
Lesser blue-eared starling
Superb starling
Yellow-billed oxpecker
Red-billed oxpecker

Violet-backed sunbird
Eastern violet-backed sunbird
Purple-banded sunbird
Copper sunbird
Miombo double-collared sunbird
Mariqua sunbird
Shelley's sunbird
Red-headed weaver
Yellow-crowned bishop
White-winged widowbird
Black-winged red bishop
Southern red bishop
Masked weaver
Golden-backed weaver
Black-necked weaver
Chestnut weaver
Vitelline masked weaver
Holub's golden weaver
Cardinal quelea
Red-billed buffalo weaver
White-headed buffalo weaver
Grey-headed sparrow weaver
Chestnut sparrow
Speckle-fronted weaver
Straw coloured whydah
Steel-blue whydah
Pin-tailed whydah
Paradise whydah
Common waxbill
Black-cheeked waxbill
Crimson-rumped waxbill
Jameson's firefinch
African firefinch
Red-billed firefinch
Orange-winged pytilia
Green-winged pytilia
Red-cheeked cordonbleu
Blue-capped cordonbleu
Cut-throat
Grey-headed silverbill
Cabanis' bunting
Golden-breasted bunting
Cinnamon rock bunting
Yellow-rumped seed-eater
Stripe-breasted seed-eater
White-bellied canary
Brimstone canary

FURTHER READING

Although there are a considerable number of subject specialised works as well as scattered academic papers on the Eastern Arc Mountains, there are very few books on Ruaha National Park. The recommended list includes:

Baker, Neil, *Bird Atlas of Tanzania* (Forthcoming. Robert Glen's Ruaha list)
Glen, Robert, *Bird checklist of Ruaha*, Friends of Ruaha, 2000
Burgess, N.D., et al, *Biodiversity of Conservation of the Eastern Arc Mountains of Kenya and Tanzania*, Morogoro, Tanzania, 1/5 December 1997
Congdon, Colin and Collins, Steve, *Butterflies of Tanzania (Supplement)*, Lambillionea, 1998
Kielland, Jan, *Butterflies of Tanzania*, Hill House, 1990
Kingdon, Jonathan, *Island Africa: The Evolution of Africa's Rare Animals and Plants*, Collins, 1990
Lovett, Jon and Wasser, Samuel, *Biogeography & Ecology of the Rain Forests of Eastern Africa*, Cambridge University Press, 1993
Mbuya, L. H. et al, *Useful Trees and Shrubs for Tanzania*, Regional Soil Conservation Unit and Swedish International Development Authority, 1994
Pennington, Ken, *Butterflies of Southern Africa*, Struik, 1994
Skinner, J. D. and Smithers, R. H. N., *The Mammals of the southern African subregion*, University of Pretoria, 1990
Snelson, Deborah, *Ruaha National Park*, Tanzania National Parks, 1991
Tanzania Forest Conservation Group, *The Arc Journal*, biannual publication

Into Africa Travel Guides (* denotes forthcoming)

Tanzania
Serengeti: Endless Plains
Ngorongoro: Book of Life
Kilimanjaro: Africa's Beacon
Zanzibar: Spice Islands
Udzungwa Mountains
Mikumi
*Arusha**
*Tarangire**
*Lake Manyara**

Mozambique
Maputo

Botswana
*Chobe**
*Okavango**

Zimbabwe
Great Zimbabwe: Houses of Stone
Victoria Falls: Mosi-oa-Tunya
Hwange: Elephant Country
Kariba: Nyaminyami's Kingdom
Harare: Sunshine City
Bulawayo: City of Kings
Bvumba: Magic in the Mist

Namibia
Windhoek
*The Skeleton Coast**
*Etosha**

Zambia
Luangwa

INDEX